The Merry Burial Compendium

Other Titles by Glenn Alan Cheney

Dr. Jamoke's Little Book of Hitherto Uncompiled
Facts and Curiosities Regarding Bees

His Hands on Earth:
Courage, Compassion, Charism,
and the Missionary Sisters of the Sacred Heart of Jesus

Quilombo dos Palmares:
Brazil's Lost Nation of Fugitive Slaves

Thanksgiving: The Pilgrims' First Year in America

Journey on the Estrada Real:
Encounters in the Mountains of Brazil

Love and Death in the Kingdom of Swaziland

How a Nation Grieves: Press Accounts of the Death of Lincoln,
the Hunt for Booth, and America in Mourning

Ex Cathedra: Stories by Machado de Assis (translator/editor)

To the Ends of the Earth (translator)

The Best Chronicles of Rubem Alves (translator)

Tender Returns (translator)

Be Revolutionary: Some Thoughts from Pope Francis

Frankenstein on the Cusp of Something

Passion in an Improper Place

The Merry Burial Compendium

Glenn Alan Cheney

New London Librarium

The Merry Burial Compendium
by Glenn Alan Cheney

Cover painting: *Dark Meadow*, by Glenn Alan Cheney

The last section of this book previously appeared in The Merry Burial Blog at ctgreenburialgrounds.org and is republished here with permission of Connecticut Green Burial Grounds.

Published by
New London Librarium
P.O. Box 284
Hanover, CT 06350
NLLibrarium.com

ISBN: 978-1-947074-04-0

Printed in the United States

to Liz

Contents

Thanatology, History, and Myth

Vernacular of Death and Burial

cadaver: a dead body, or corpse, especially one to be used for dissection or research.

cadaverine: the foul-smelling chemical produced by the putrefaction of animal tissue.

cairn: a mound of stones atop a grave.

casket: a burial or cremation container, generally rectangular or oval in shape. (see *coffin*)

catacomb: a human-made underground passageway or system of underground spaces for religious ceremonies or burials.

cenotaph: an empty tomb or monument established in honor of a deceased person who is not buried there, sometimes the initial tomb of a person who was buried there but removed.

chippie: a coffin or casket made of particle board, generally used for cremation.

coffin: strictly defined, a burial container usually with six sides, i.e. with "shoulders" narrowing to the head area. The term is often considered synonymous with the four-sided *casket*.

columbarium niche: a cemetery plot reserved for burial of cremated remains.

cremains: a person's cremated remains; considered by some to be a disrespectful term.

crematorium: a facility with crematory units and possibly offering related services.

cremator: the part of a crematorium where bodies are cremated; also known as a crematory.

cremulator: a British term for the machine somewhat like a blender that pulverizes cremated remains into the "ashes" that are delivered to a client.

crematory: the part of a crematorium where bodies are cremated, also known as a cremator.

crypt: a stone chamber beneath a church or other building for the interment of the dead or religious relics.

death anxiety: the fear of dying.

death, brain: the absence of electrical activity in the brain and the complete cessation of brain function, including all involuntary actions such as breathing, sustaining of body temperature, etc. It is synonymous with cerebral death, though definitions vary. It may or may not include brain stem death. The bodily functions of a brain-dead body can be sustained by artificial means.

death, clinical: the cessation of blood circulation and breathing, also known as cardiopulmonary death. Clinical death can be reversed.

death doula: a person who assists in the process of dying; also known as a death midwife.

decedent: a deceased person.

diener: a person responsible for moving, cleaning, and assisting in the embalming or autopsy of a corpse.

DNR: An acronym of Do Not Resuscitate, a DNR is a binding decision by an individual to not to be resuscitated by medical intervention if breathing or heartbeat have stopped.

inter: to place in a grave or tomb

interment: burial.

martyrium: a mausoleum for the remains of a martyr.

mausoleum: a building enclosing an interment space or burial chamber. A mausoleum may be considered a type of tomb or the enclosure of a tomb.

metempsychosis: the transmigration of the soul to some kind of reincarnated existence.

morgue: a place where a body is stored pending transfer or burial.

mortuary: a morgue or funeral home.

necrophobia: fear of the dead and things associated with death, such as tombs or coffins (not necessarily of dying).

psychopom: Greek for *soul guide*, a creature, angel, or spirit of some sort that escorts the dead to the afterlife.

pyre: a structure, usually of wood, with the purpose of burning a body as part of a funeral rite.

rainbow's end: a British euphemism for a mortuary.

resomation: the alkaline hydrolysis process of cremating a body with lye under pressure, resulting in the body being broken down into chemical compounds.

retort: the firing chamber where a body is cremated.

rose cottage: a British euphemism for a mortuary.

sarcophagus: A stone container for a body, coffin, or casket, often decorated as part of a monument or mausoleum.

sati: self-immolation ritual in which a widowed woman throws herself on her deceased husband's pyre.

scaphism: (You do not want to know.)

sepulcher: a space carved from rock for the interment of a body.

sky burial: the disposal of a body by leaving in the open air—on the ground or on a platform—for consumption by animals.

taxidermy: the recreation of an animal's form often using only the creature's skin mounted on an anatomical form (as opposd to embalming, which preserves much of the body).

thanatology: the study of death.

thanatophilia: necrophilia, the sexual atttraction to or sexual act with a corpse.

thanatophobia: fear of death or dying

tumulus: a burial mound, the mound of dirt atop a grave, a barrow. (see also *cairn*).

Unspeakable Love

Necrophilia is the sexual attraction to corpses. The rare disorder includes *regular necrophilia* (the use of dead bodies for sexual purposes), *necrophilic fantasy* (fantasizing about sex with bodies), *necrophilic homicide* (murder to acquire a body for sexual purposes), and *pseudonecrophilia,* transient, usually opportunistic sexual contact with bodies).

No one knows how common necrophilia is. Due to people's extreme reluctance to admit to the practice or even related fantasies, it is impossible to even estimate its prevalence. It is known to have happened throughout history. Greek historian Herodotus reported that the deceased wives of men of rank would not be sent for embalming for several days lest the embalmers violate them. The Catholic Church felt it was enough of a problem that it needed its own category. It wasn't whoring ("fornicatio") or bestiality. It was "pollution with a tendency to whoring."

The rare cases that are known are almost always because someone was caught doing it. It is supposed that many necrophilic fantasizers are reluctant to admit their fantasies.

A study published in the Bulletin of the American Academy of Psychiatry and the Law (J. Rosman and P. Resnick, June, 1989) reviewed 88 documented and 34 undocumented cases. Of this limited number, 92% were male. In cases where sexuality was known, 79% were heterosexual, 13% were bisexual, and 9% were homosexual. Twenty-six percent were married, and 14% were divorced or widowed. Most had professional access to corpses. Eighty percent of fantasizers consumed alcohol before the act. The most common motivation was a desire for an unresisting, unrejecting partner. Second was reunion with a romantic partner. Fifteen percent were simply attracted to corpses.

Don't Worry about It

Death Anxiety is the fear of dying. You'd be nuts if you didn't feel it but downright abnormal if you let it paralyze you the way anxiety can do.

It's also called thanatophobia, named after the Greek reaper Thanatos.

Death anxiety has been around since people were amoebas, back when we first learned to sense danger and do something about it. Basically, we've learned to run away or fight back. As we became human, of course, things got complicated. Endowed with a sense of guilt, we learned to take on a fear of death after causing someone else's death. When we figured out that no matter what we do, we're going to die, we invented, by psychological necessity, denial.

Freud theorized that thanatophobia isn't really a fear of death. He theorized that people cannot fear death because they can't imagine it, have never experienced it, and can't really believe that they will die. An apparent fear of death, he said, is really a subconscious anxiety about some kind of unresolved problem in childhood. The problem may have nothing to do with death, but it sure feels like death is behind it.

Everyone Is Dying

The mortality rate of human beings continues to be one hundred percent. Approximately 150,000 people die each day. About two thirds of them basically get old and die. In industrialized countries, that portion may reach 90 percent of deaths. In developing countries, infectious diseases are the leading cause of death. In industrial countries, it's heart disease and other diseases relating to obesity and old age. Malaria kills between one million and three million per year. Tuberculosis kills about 1.8 million. Tobacco is expected to kill a billion people in the 21st century. In 2012, suicide surpassed traffic accidents as the leading cause of death by injury in the United States, where people spend some $500 billion per year on anti-aging products that have never been proven effective.

Grim and Screaming Reapers

In ancient Brittany, the Breton people feared the Ankou, a version of the Grim Reaper who was not a skeleton with a scythe but the last person in the community who had died. He or she might appear as a skeleton or as an old, worn-out person with broad-brimmed hat and long, white hair. The Ankou drove a wagon stacked with corpses, stopping at the house of the imminently dead. One could hear the axle of the Ankou's cart creaking as it approached. One could only hope the creaking didn't stop.

Back in the days of leprechauns and shillelaghs, people feared the scream of a banshee. A banshee was a mythological female spirit who cut loose with a blood-curdling shriek in front of someone's house. Sometimes she looked like an old witch. (The Welsh feared a similar figure, but she was known as the Hag of the Mist.) Sometimes she looked like a sweet young girl. In either case she was probably wearing red or green, and her hair might look like it was on fire. She might wail a mournful tune as a harbinger of death, or she might screech loud enough to not only break a window but push somebody over the edge. A pack of banshees outside your house would be a recognition that you were a great person and would be remembered as such.

During the scourge of the Black Plague of the 14th century, the Norse were never happy to see the Plague Hag come to town. They knew her as Pesta, a word related to the English *pest* and *pestilence*. Pesta looked like she was in the Reaper family, but instead of a scythe she carried either a rake or a broom. If a rake, the bad news was a little good—at least some people in town would survive the plague. But if she brought a broom, she'd be sweeping the place clean.

The Nice Guy from Hell

Osiris was the Egyptian god of death and the underworld. But as death deities go, he was actually a rather positive figure. Through him, death was associated with resurrection and regeneration, the very cycles of life. As a merciful judge of the dead, he was grantor of all birth, including that of plants arising from his underworld.

Glenn Alan Cheney

An Underworld of Greek Gods

Hades was the Greek god-king of the Underworld which eventually took on his name. In time, as cultures mixed, he was assumed to be the same as the Etruscan god Aita and two Roman gods, Dis Pater and Orcus. They merged and became known as Plouton, whose name became Pluto in Rome. While the name Hades was known for provoking fear, Pluto was associated with wealth because wealth was seen as emanating from underground in the form of precious metals, gems, and crops.

Hades ruled, but he did not rule alone. Other gods of the Underworld include his wife Persephone, whom Hades abducted because they were meant for each other, she being the goddess of seeds and vegetation, he being the god of the place where seeds sprout. Still, it was a complicated relationship that began with rape. Thanatos (spirit of death), Rhadamantus, Minos and Aeacus (judges of the dead), Angelos (a daughter of Zeus, whose realm was the sky), Menoetes (herdsman of Hades' cattle), Orphne (one of the Lampades nymphs who carried torches, hence our word *lamp*), Erebus (god of darkness), the Keres (goddesses of violent death), Lamia (Underworld vampire), a god or goddess for each of the seven rivers of the Underworld (the most famous being the goddess Styx), Charon (ran the ferry across the Styx), the Erinyes (gods of vengeance), Clotho (who spun the thread of life), Lachesis (who measured the thread allotted to each person), and Atropos (who cut the thread, ending life).

The Other St. Joseph

St. Joseph of Arimathea is the patron saint of undertakers. All four Gospels mention him. He was a wealthy businessman who dealt in metals. (It is mere coincidence that metals as a source of wealth are associated with Pluto, Roman god of the Underworld, where metals come from.) It was Joseph who, on the first Good Friday, went to Pontius Pilate to ask permission to recover the body of Jesus from the Cross. Joseph prepared the body for burial, anointed it with oils, shrouded it in linen, and carried it to the cave where he was so briefly interred. Joseph is remembered for his courage and kindness.

The Bible says no more about Joseph, but according to legend, Joseph had taken the youngster Jesus to the Isle of Britain on a business trip, which accounts for the gap on Jesus' résumé between his childhood and his ministry. Years later, Joseph is said to have returned to Glastonbury with the Holy Grail, the cup he had used to catch the blood from the crucified Christ. William Blake immortalized the legend in his poem Jerusalem, which includes the quatrain

> And did those feet in ancient time
> Walk upon England's mountains green?
> And was the holy Lamb of God
> On England's pleasant pastures seen?

Is it coincidence that the Saint's Day of St. Joseph of Arimathea's is March 17, the same as that of St. Patrick, patron saint of the Irish who populate so much of the American funeral industry? Just maybe.

Saints Preserved

The remains of several saints and beati of the Roman Catholic Church have been exhumed and reported to have not decomposed. In some cases, the bodies were accompanied by an aroma of holiness described as sweet or floral. The inexplicable preservation is attributed to the "incorruptibility" of truly holy individuals. This is not to say that none of the bodies of saints have decomposed, but when they don't, it is confirmation of holiness.

In some cases, decomposition was somehow avoided despite conditions which would normally hasten it. A classic example was St. Francis Xavier. He was first buried on the beach of tropical Shangchuan Island. It was dug up six months later and found uncorrupted by decomposition. He was the moved to Malacca, where he was buried for about a month. Then he was dug up and shipped to tropical Goa. His right forearm was removed and sent to Rome. Another arm was sent to Macao. The rest of the body remains in a glass case in a silver casket in Goa, as fresh as a mutilated daisy that's been dead for half a millennium.

Preservation due to embalming, mummification, lack of oxygen, or other explanations is not considered incorruptibility.

Corpses and Cadavers

Dat Great Brick House

Was it folklore, disinformation, or reality? In the days of American slavery, blacks feared "Night Doctors" who sought cadavers—especially those of people who had neither voice nor right to life—for dissection and experimentation. These weren't necessarily corpses dug up from graves, which at the time was the only source of corpses used for experimental and training purposes. According to tales, if not verifiable reports, white doctors or their agents would abduct blacks, take them to some kind of medical facility, snuff them, and use their bodies for dissection. Blacks knew them as Night Riders, Night Witches, KKK Doctors, and Student Doctors. Historians say these were only vicious rumors generated by slave owners and, after Emancipation, white farm owners who wanted to discourage migration to the north. Men in white gowns would prowl around Afro-American communities, pretending to be looking for eligible victims. White people who wouldn't be missed—sailors in port, immigrants, indigents— could also find themselves on a slab in a classroom or operating amphitheater.

In the 1830s, the Transylvania University Medical Department in Lexington, KY, lost prestige for lack of corpses. Nearby Louisville Medical Institute, located where there were more blacks and transients, had no such problem.

The Medical College of Georgia in Augusta bought Grandison Harris for the purpose of janitorial work and the procurement of black corpses, which he did for 50 years, robbing graves and otherwise procuring specimens.

Whether doctors and students acquired black corpses by abducting living people is not known. But blacks and whites both ended up on dissecting tables, which is interesting in that blacks were considered something other than human while alive. Once dead, they were human enough.

The following poem, apparently written by a white imitating black dialect and making fun of black fears, was propagated in the late 19th or early 20th century:

THE DISSECTING HALL

Yuh see dat house? Dat great brick house?
Way yonder down de street?
Dey used to take dead folks een dar
Wrapped een a long white sheet.
An' sometimes we'en a nigger' d stop,
A-wondering who was dead,
Dem stujent men would take a club
An' bat 'im on de head.
An' drag dat poor dead nigger chile
Right een dat 'sectin hall
To vestigate 'is liver-lights-
His gizzardan' 'is gall.
Tek off dat nigger's han's an' feet-
His eyes, his head, an' all,
An' w'en dem stujent finish
Dey was nothin' left at all.

Burke: transitive verb

Until 1832, the only legal source of cadavers for medical and educational purposes in England was the bodies of criminals condemned to not only death but dissection. The death sentence might be imposed for relatively light crimes, while dissection was reserved for murderers. Dissection was allowed on these individuals because Christians believed that dissected bodies could not rise to Heaven, a place the worst criminals were not expected to go. But there weren't enough heinous crimes to supply the demand, so grave robbing—a mere misdemeanor—became common.

Bodysnatchers used wooden shovels because they were quieter than metal. They would dig a hole at the head-end of the grave until they reached the coffin. They would break the coffin open, put a rope around the corpse, and haul it out through the hole. Then they would replace the turf so that no one would notice the theft.

Disturbing the dead was, of course, frowned upon by those who had no use for cadavers, especially those of their dearly departed. To prevent theft, some families had iron cages constructed around graves. Others guarded the graves at night until the body was decomposed beyond scientific use. Thefts were less common in the summer because decomposition took place more quickly. October to May was bodysnatching season.

Inevitably, astute bodysnatchers figured out it would be easier to skip the digging process by gently murdering people and selling the fresh, undamaged corpses. Thus the English language acquired the transitive verb *burke*—to execute by suffocation so as to leave the body intact for dissection. The word is derived from William Burke, who burked 16 people. He was tried, found guilty, and in 1828 hanged before a crowd of 25,000, then publicly dissected. His skeleton now resides at the Anatomical Museum of Edinburgh Medical School, and his verb resides in the Oxford English Dictionary.

Family Dental Practice

British dentist Martin van Butchell wasn't one to let a good wife go to waste. When his beloved Mary passed away in 1775, he saw opportunity where others saw mere death. He hired a couple of shady anatomists to embalm poor Mary, preserving her in as life-like a state as possible. They injected her cheeks with coloring to give them a warm rosiness, replaced her eyes with glass eyeballs, and dressed her in the finest lace that any wife of a dentist could ask for. They they caked her with plaster and tucked her into a glass-topped coffin.

Dr. Butchell put his wife on display in his office window. She looked pretty good, for a dead lady. She attracted many onlookers and made quite a name for her widower. Whether he succeeded in attracting more or fewer dental patients is not known. He did manage to attract a new wife, Elizabeth, but she insisted that the ex- in the window had to go. Butchell gave Mary to a museum, and she eventually ended up at the Royal College of Surgeons. Mary's remains did not weather the next century and a half very well. A German bombing raid in 1941 finally put her out of her posthumous misery.

The Truth about the Kadaververwertungsanstalt

During the First World War, various newspapers reported that a factory, called the Kadaververwertungsanstalt, was rendering German battlefield corpses into fat. The fat was then used to manufacture candles, soap, lubricants, boot wax, and even the explosive nitroglycerine. Rumors of the factory were rife in the English trenches, bolstering the belief that defeating Germany was worth all the suffering.

But it seems something was lost—or, more aptly put, enhanced—in translation. The original report appeared in a German newspaper, which did indeed refer to a factory that rendered *"kadavers."* The story was only 59 words long and was about the smell of the place, not the bodies. A Belgian newspaper then expanded the story to 500 words, enhancing it with descriptions of a deep forest, an electrified fence, and soap of a yellowish-brown color. Another Belgian paper expanded on that, and then The Times of London and The Daily Mail picked it up.

It wasn't until after the war that someone noted that *kadaver* in German refers to the body of an animal, rarely a human.

Adolf Hitler later used the English reports as evidence that British papers cannot be trusted to tell the truth. But it may have given him an idea. During World War II, Nazis experimented with rendering people into soap, reportedly producing 25 kg of soap from the fat of 40 people. Despite rumors to the contrary, the process was never taken to industrial scale.

Apocryphal Anthropodermia

Did Nazis really make anthropodermic lampshades from the skin of murdered Jews? No. It was alleged that Ilse Koch, "The Bitch of Buchenwald," wife of the commandant of that concentration camp, had lampshades of skin, but at her post-war trial it was determined that the lampshades were made with the skin of goats. But that doesn't mean nobody ever made a lampshade of human skin.

The apocryphal report from Buchenwald inspired Edward Theodore Gein, an American murderer and bodysnatcher, to include a lampshade among many items he crafted from human parts, among them a wastebasket, seat covers, bowls, leggings, masks, and a corset.

And then there's anthropodermic bibliopegy—the use of human skin to bind books. Seventeen such books are known to exist, and several more are allegedly human though quite possibly of animals. Part of the binding of a copy of Dale Carnegie's *Lincoln the Unknown* is said to have been "taken from the skin of a Negro at a Baltimore Hospital and tanned by the Jewell Belting Company."

Dummies Beat the Dead

Among the many good deeds performed by the deceased has been the improvement of car safety. Crash dummies are fine for certain experiments, but there's nothing like the real thing. Only a cadaver can demonstrate soft tissue damage. In one experiment, seat belts seemed to to do their job well, but only with dummies. When actual cadavers were put to the test, it was found that the seat belt protected the thorax but not the pelvis. Crash dummies had failed that test because they do not have moving parts in the pelvic area. But no body's perfect. It's hard to get cadavers to sit up straight.

FUNERALS AND BURIAL

Cemeterial Behavior

What kind of behavior is appropriate for a cemetery? Should people be allowed to jog or do other kinds of exercise? Should families be allowed to picnic? If so, should their picnic space be allowed to infringe on the grace space of unrelated people? How about a barbecue grill? Should a lawn tractor be allowed to drive over a grave? How long may a maintenance person operate a weed-whacker, leaf-blower, or other loud machinery? Should children be allowed to play hide-and-seek behind gravestones? Should people be allowed to plant flowers on their loved-one's grave? How about a bush? How about a tree? How about leaving plastic flowers on a grave? How about flags other than American flags? Should it be permissible to leave things on the graves of strangers? Should the consumption of alcohol be allowed? Why not allow smoking? Are firearms OK? Can they be shot into the sky? How about fireworks? Should cemeteries be open after dark? Why shouldn't someone be able to camp out on the grave of a loved one? Should commercial solicitation be allowed? How about religious prosyletizing? How about begging?

Should freedom of speech be in any way limited? Is it constitutional to prohibit anti-war protestors from shouting during the funeral of a combat veteran? Was it OK for a union to inflate a giant rat just outside a funeral that was using a non-union-made coffin?

Who should make these decisions? A private cemetery association? A municipality? The federal government? The families of the deceased? Those present at a funeral in process? Or no one?

Just in Case

Taphophobia is the fear of being buried alive. And it's not an unfounded fear. "Premature burial" has been known to happen.

Given the horror of slowly expiring in the dark of a tight space, coffins have been designed for the possibility of escape. One had a pipe that allowed air into the buried coffin and which could be moved to indicate life below. A vault in Williamsport, PA, had a hatch through which the resurrected could escape. Duke Ferdinand of Brunswick had a window on his coffin that would fog over if he exhaled. A german priest invented a coffin with a trumpet-like tube where he could sniff for putrefaction (or rather, the lack of it) or hear anyone calling for help. There were coffins with strings attached to bells or flags aboveground, coffins with bellows allowing the interred to pump in air, a coffin with an emergency alarm, an intercom system, and a heart monitor.

Despite the popularity of these "safe coffins," there has never been a case of the prematurely interred signaling life.

From the New York Times, February 21, 1885

Asheville, N.C., Feb. 20.—A gentleman from Flat Creek Township in this (Buncombe) County, furnishes the information that about the 20th of last month a young man by the name of Jenkins, who had been sick with fever for several weeks, was thought to have died. He became speechless, his flesh was cold and clammy, and he could not be roused, and there appeared to be no action of the pulse and heart. He was thought to be dead and was prepared for burial, and it was noticed at that time there was no stiffness in any of the limbs. He was buried the day after his supposed death, and when put in the coffin it was remarked that he was as limber as a live man. There was much talk in the neighborhood about the case, and the opinion was frequently expressed that Jenkins had been buried alive. Nothing, however, was done about the matter until the 10th inst., when the coffin was taken up for the purpose of removal and interment in the family burying ground in Henderson Country. The coffin, being wood, it was suggested that it be opened in order to see if the body was in such condition that it could be hauled 20 miles without being put in a metallic casket. The coffin was opened, and to the great astonishment and horror of his relatives the body was lying face downward, the hair had been pulled from the head in great quantities, and there were scratches of the finger nails on the inside of the lid and side of the coffin. These facts caused great excitement and all acquainted personally with the facts believe Jenkins was in a trance, or that animation was apparently suspended, and that he was not really dead when buried, and that he returned to consciousness only to find himself buried and beyond help. The body was then taken to Henderson Country and reinterred. The relatives are so distressed beyond measure at what they term criminal carelessness in not being absolutely sure Jenkins was dead before he was buried.

Burial in the Air

No "safe coffinms" are needed for a sky burial. In a sky burial, the corpse is expeditiously introduced into the lifecycle by allowing it to be consumed by birds, especially vultures. It has been practiced by Buddhists in East Asia, from Bhutan and Tibet to China and Mongolia for thousands of years, but a suspected sky burial site some 4,500 years old has also been identified at Stonehenge. Zoroastrians also practice sky burial.

In a sky burial, the corpse is left in the open, above ground, often high on a mountain. The practice is appropriate for places with a lack of firewood for cremation and ground that is too rocky for the digging of a grave. The body may be left on an elevated platform or high rock, or just left on the ground. Since many such burials are practiced in the same place, vultures are often waiting. They know what to do.

Transmigration of spirits is an essential belief in Buddhism. Buddhists believe that once the spirit has left the body, there is no need to preserve the body. In fact, giving the body to living beings is seen as an act of generosity by the deceased, a virtue of the religion. The process is believed to make it easier for the spirit to abandon the body and move on to the next life.

In Tibet, vultures are given all the time they need to consume all the flesh of the body. The body is then dismantled, the bones mashed with mallets, then ground up with barley, yak butter, or milk. The mixture is then fed to the crows and hawks who were waiting for the vultures to leave.

Some regions suffer a shortage of vultures. They can't consume all the bodies offered on a given day. This is bad news for a spirit trying to leave one body and find another. Ritual dances are performed to increase the appetite.

Other regions have too many vultures, and they're very eager to get their beaks into the deceased. Sometimes people involved in the funeral rites have to fend them off with sticks.

Saving the Bones

Excarnation is the practice of removing the flesh and organs from a corpse before burial—is a time-honored rite that goes back to the neolithic era. Tibetans and Zoroastrians do it. Comanches used to do it. Medieval Christians did it if the deceased was of high enough status. Hawaiians did it to Captain Cook because they thought he was a god.

By his personal request, Christopher Columbus was excarnated after he died in 1506 in Valladolid, Spain. Even in death he was a traveling man. At his request, his bones were stripped of flesh, an illegal process known as excarnation. The flesh was disposed of and the bones were buried in Valladolid. The bones were soon dug up and moved to a monastery in southern Spain. But Columbus had asked that his bones be buried in Santo Domingo, so in fifteen hundred and forty two, Columbus sailed the ocean blue all the way to the island that he had "discovered." When the French took over the island, Columbus's remains made a quick sail across the Caribbean blue to Havana, where he would be safely in Spanish territory. When Cuba fell to American invaders in 1898, Columbus crossed the deep blue again, this time to rest in Seville, where his remains remain within a silver model of a ship on a magnificent catafalque.

Carion Baggage

Mos Teutonicus was the medieval practice of excarnating flesh from the bones of men killed in battle so their bones could be shipped home. This avoided the problem of shipping a decomposing body over long distances.

The Germans started the practice during the Crusades. Then other Christian nations started doing it. Their aristocratic leaders didn't want to be buried in Muslim territory, but their men didn't want to lug their rotting bodies back to Germany.

The solution was to dismember the body so its parts would fit in a kettle. The entrails, which were seen as something disgusting, were left in the unholy land as a kind of insult. The rest of the body was boiled in water or wine until the flesh slid off their bones. But the flesh had to go home, so they salted it as they would any other meat they wished to preserve.

This is how French King Louis IX came from Tunis. This went on until Pope Boniface VIII, who believed God did not want humans to be cut up, issued a papal bull prohibiting the practice. For many years his edict was misinterpreted as a prohibition against dissection of cadavers. The misunderstanding did much to hold back the advance of science.

Burial in the Water

Burial at sea is a "green" burial that quickly introduces a corpse to an ecological system.

Most religions allow burial at sea under certain circumstances, but none require it. The Catholic Church prefers burial in the ground and in a casket. Cremation is allowed if the ashes are buried or entombed. It does not allow the scattering of ashes on land or at sea. Burial at sea in a casket or urn is allowed only when a person has died at sea. The rationale is that friends and family need a specific, identifiable, sacred place where they can visit the deceased.

Protestant churches generally have no prohibition against burial at sea. Some have special prayers for such burials.

Hindus prefer to cremate a corpse, then disperse the ashes and other remains in a river, ideally the sacred Ganges, but any river will do.

Islam prefers burial in the ground but allows burial at sea when death occurs on a ship. (An exception was made for Osama bin Laden.) The body is to be weighted at the feet and lowered into the water, preferably where there are no sharks.

Judaism requires burial in the ground on the day of death, in accordance with instruction found in Deuteronomy. If death occurs at sea or anywhere else where the body threatens the health of others but cannot be buried, the principle of pikuach nefesh can be invoked to what must be done.

The United States allows full-body burial at sea only in areas at least 3.5 miles from land in water at least 600 feet deep. The body or casket must be prepared so as to sink immediately. Off the coast of New England, a ship or plane would have to go some 45 miles out to sea to find suitable depth. A trip off Miami may be as short as five miles. Individual states have various rules on the scattering of ashes in the sea. California, for example, does not allow cremated remains within 500 feet of shore, and the remains must be removed from any urn unless it's a specialized "scattering urn" that will disperse ashes within four hours.

The Navy Way

Navies perform burial at sea when necessary, especially during times of war. The United States Navy offers free burial at sea—regardless of the place of death—to active, retired, and honorably discharged personnel, civilian Sealift Command personnel, and the families of such veterans.

Naval burials are performed with the ship stopped, its flags at half mast. The crew assembles on deck, initially at parade rest. If the body is in a coffin, it is covered with a flag, carried feet-first and set on a platform with feet toward the sea. In wartime, the body may be shrouded in sailcloth and weighted with rocks or cannonballs. If ashes are in an urn, the urn is placed on a special stand. A military ceremony precedes a religious ceremony, the latter performed by a chaplain or, if necessary, the commanding officer. The firing party is then ordered to present arms, and the crew is called to attention. The casket is slid into the sea, with the flag remaining on board. If the deceased has been reduced to ashes, either the urn can be dropped into the sea or the ashes can be scattered, with all due attention to wind direction.

The firing party fires a three-volley salute. A bugler plays taps. The flag is folded, and with that, the ceremony ends. Relatives are informed of the time and location, and they may be presented with photographs or video recordings.

Burial in Reef

Once an author and television chef, Julia Child is now part of a reef off the coast of south Florida. Some years ago she arranged to have The Neptune Society mix her ashes with concrete and sink her personalized chunk in an artificial reef forty feet below the surface of the sea. Many other people have done the same. Divers take their blocks to spots that people chose before they died.

The Neptune Society Memorial Reef isn't just a reef. It's an artsy, fantasized representation of Atlantis. It's also the largest artificial reef in the world. It stands where there was once just barren ocean floor. Though the ashes of the deceased are locked out of the life cycle for a long, long time, the concrete blocks form part of a habitat for all sorts of sea life. The reef has already sprouted coral colonies and attracted several species of fish, including a sea urchin previously thought to be extinct. The reef also attracts recreational scuba divers, marine biologists, researchers and ecologists. Among the divers are family members of the deceased. Anyone is welcome to visit, but fishing is strictly prohibited.

Burial in Wood

The Moriori people of Chatham Island, today part of New Zealand, disposed of the deceased in several ways, indicating that their ancestral background is populated by various cultures. One method was described in a paper presented to the Wellington Philosophical Society:

"In some instances the corpses were placed upright between young trees, and then firmly bound round with vines, and in course of time they became embedded in the wood itself; sometimes they were placed in hollow trees. Several skeletons have lately been discovered by Europeans in trees which they were cutting up for firewood, &c."

Burial in Woods

A cemetery in Germany is based on "forest burials." People can "buy" an existing tree and have their ashes buried beneath it in a biodegradable urn. People are opting for forest burial not just for ecological reasons but because they won't have to depend on cemetery maintenance people or renew their ownership of a grave every 20 years. The cost of a tree depends on species and size. A small beech might cost EUR 3,350 (USD 3,900). A tall oak with broad crown could run UR 6,000 (USD 7,000). There are options for family trees, friendship trees, and community trees. A tree can be marked with a small sign that may bear a name, a saying, a verse from the Bible, or a Christian symbol.

When Journalism was Art

The following "found poem" was originally a paragraph in the April 25, 1865 edition of the Philadelphia newspaper The Age. The article described the showing of Abraham Lincoln's body during a brief stop on its journey to Springfield, Illinois. The paragraph was rendered word-for-word into a poem published in *How a Nation Grieves: Press Accounts of the Death of Lincoln, the Hunt for Booth, and America in Mourning.*

Every article in the room bore evidences
of the burden and heat of the day,
and shared in the purifying attentions.

The flowers filled with dust,
and their white and crimson mouths,
instead of being filled with soft silver dew,

were dry and parched and arid,
sprinkled over with dust, as though
it had been distributed by a dredger box.

The wax tapers were discolored with it,
and it seemed even to make the flames
of the candles sputter.

It had settled in thick layers
upon the portion of the coffin lid
which had not been removed, and,

above all, on the features of the dead.

This it was, the dusty accumulation
of a whole day, which lent so leaden
a cast to the face,

and covered with an unruffled
and unnatural veil the really
genial and kind expression.

But the undertaker's skillful brush,
long, thick, light, and flossy,
removed, with a few artistic touches,

the unseemly discoloration,
and a white cambric handkerchief, delicately applied,
transformed to itself the last molecule lingerings.

Islamic Burial Rites

The grave is dug at an angle perpendicular to the direction of Mecca. The gravediggers roll and pack tight three fist-sized dirt balls. The body is ritually washed an odd number of times by family members of the same gender. Then the body, wrapped in a shroud of simple cloth—white cotton preferred—is laid on its right side, facing Mecca. A male relative places the dirt balls under the deceased's chin, head, and shoulders as props. Then each person present contributes three handfuls of soil into the grave while reciting "We created you from it, and return you into it, and from it we will raise you a second time." Lavish displays are discouraged—a wreath will do— and wailing is not permitted.

Jewish Burial Rites

After the body is cleansed, it is dressed in burial clothing, including a prayer shawl if the deceased had used one. One fringe from the shawl is removed to signify that the deceased no longer needs to pray or keep the commandments. If the body is to be buried in a casket, it must be stripped of all linings and embellishments. Family members scatter soil on the body and around the casket. The preferred soil comes from Eretz, Israel. In Israel, caskets are used only for those worthy of great honor. Others are wrapped in a shroud. Mourners take turns adding a shovel of soil to the grave. They turn the shovel over to represent life overcoming death. To avoid passing their grief to the next in line, they stick the shovel in the earth rather than hand it on. The date of death is commemorated each year with the lighting of a candle.

When in Palermo

Feel like a ghoulish tour? If so, the Capuchin Catacombs of Palermo is the place to go.

The catacombs have been there since the 16th century, when the Capuchin monastery cemetery ran out of room. To create more space, the friars began excavating caves behind the altar of the Church of Santa Maria della Pace. During the excavation, expired friars were stored in an underground charnel house. When the first catacomb was ready, the friars exhumed their fallen members and found, to their shock and awe, that 45 friars had barely decomposed. Their faces were still recognizable! It had to be a miracle, one of God's many mysterious ways.

The friars took it as a sign that they should not bury the corpses. Rather, the remains should be kept on display as relics of the miracle. They propped the bodies in niches along the catacomb walls.

The friars continued to store their dead in this way, embalming or mummifying them as best they could. They first dehydrated bodies by letting them dry out on ceramic racks for a good year. Then they washed the bodies with vinegar and dressed them in something appropriate for eternity. During epidemics, they bathed the bodies with arsenic, which did an even better job of preservation.

So lay people—especially rich lay people who could afford embalming—requested that they, too be mummified and put on display. A preserved body became a status symbol, the ultimate in dignity. In 1783, the catacombs were opened to anyone who requested interment there.

The place grew to house some 8,000 corpses and 1,252 mummies. The state of the remains varies from grotesque skeletons in formal clothes or priestly frocks to the beautifully preserved body of a two-year-old Sicilian girl named Rosalia Lombardo. Rosalia died of pneumonia in 1920. Despite the passage of nearly a century, she looks as if she's alive and merely sleeping.

Researchers found the hand-written notes of the embalmer (and taxidermist) who preserved the girl's remains. He had injected her with formalin, zinc salts, alcohol, salicylic acid, and glycerin.

Formalin is a mixture of formaldehyde and water that kills bacteria in the body. The alcohol dried the girl's body, allowing it to mummify. The glycerin kept her from drying out too much. The salicylic acid prevented the growth of fungus.

All of these chemicals are still used by embalmers, but it was the zinc salts—no longer in use—that did the trick. The zinc petrified the body, preserving it perfectly. It also made her as rigid as stone. If you leaned her against a tree, she'd stand there with no other support.

The catacombs are now open to tourists (not for interment, just for a tour). You can visit every day of the year. No, you can't take pictures, touch the dead, or eat anything. In fact, you probably shouldn't even think about eating anything. Turn your cell phone, keep your voice low, and, please, leave no trash behind.

The Ways They Went

Pliny tells us that Aeschylus stayed outdoors a lot because it had been prophesied that he would be killed by a falling object. Valerius Maximus tells us Aeschylus was killed by a tortoise that an eagle had dropped, mistaking the playwright's head for a rock.

From 1 Maccabees:

> "Eleazar, called Avaran, saw one of the beasts covered with royal armor and bigger than any of the others, and so he thought the king was on it. He gave up his life to save his people and win an everlasting name for himself. He dashed courageously up to it in the middle of the phalanx, killing men right and left, so that they parted before him. He ran under the elephant, stabbed it and killed it. The beast fell to the ground on top of him, and he died there."

Crown Prince Philip of France died while riding his horse through Paris. His horse tripped over a black pig that dashed out of a dung heap.

Hans Steininger, burgomaster of Braunau, usually kept his 4.5 foot beard rolled up in a leather pouch. But one day he didn't. He tripped over it, fatally breaking his neck.

In 1919, 21 Bostonians were killed by a wave of molasses after a huge storage tank burst.

In 2007, Humberto Hernandez was killed by a fire hydrant while walking down a street. A car had collided with the hydrant, and water pressure shot it directly at Hernandez.

In Caratinga, Brazil, João Maria de Souza was killed in bed when a cow fell through his roof. The cow had stepped onto the roof from an adjacent hillside. Neither the cow nor de Souza's wife, who was in the same bed, were injured.

In 1912, Franz Reichelt, a creative tailor, fell to his death from the Eiffel Tower as he tested his invention, the parachute coat. It was his first experiment with the invention, and he had promised authorities that his first test would be with a dummy.

In 1911, famed Tennessee distiller Jack Daniels died after kicking a safe that refused to open. The kick broke open a toe which became infected and led to his death.

Down the Drain

When New York State proposed changing the definition of "cremation," the New York Catholic Conference objected. The Conference feared that a new definition might result in undignified disposal of bodies.

The new definition was to include "chemical digestion." One such digestive process is alkaline hydrolysis, also known as resomation and biocremation. The process involved submersing a body in water and lye in an airtight container and heating it to 320°F. The container is a kind of pressure cooker that lets water heat above the boiling point without actually boiling. In about three hours, the body breaks down into chemical components—greenish-brownish sludge and bone remains soft enough to crush by hand. Filtered solids are normally returned to kin. The greenish-brownish liquid can be spread on cropland or drained into the sewer system. That latter fate, a patently undignified treatment of human remains, is what disturbed the Catholic Conference.

The bill to redefine "cremation" in New York never passed, but the process is legal in about a dozen other states.

Australians are trying to make the concept more palatable by changing the name to the more pleasant-sounding "aquamation."

Environmentalists are also less than enthusiastic about resomation. While it uses less energy and thus releases less carbon dioxide (and no mercury) into the atmosphere, it still involves quite a bit of heat. A "green burial" without coffin has a much smaller carbon footprint and an passing more conducive to re-entry into the ecosystem.

None Dare Call It Care

Here's an idea for putting your mortal remains to good use, though its time may have passed. In May 2017, shortly after the House of Representatives passed a bill that would kill and replace the Affordable "ObamaCare" Care Act. Opponents charged that the replacement, the Republican-supported American "TrumpCare" Healthcare Act, would effectively kill (and not replace) thousands, if not millions, of Americans by denying them affordable health insurance.

Nicole Silverberg tweeted her response: "If I die because of TrumpCare, mail my body to Paul Ryan's house."

That gave American University junior Zoey Jordan Salsbury an idea. She set up a website: mailmetothegop.com.

At the site people could file their request to be cremated and then have their ashes mailed to the Capitol or a favorite Republican representative. Within a day, hundreds of people responded—so many that the site kept crashing with excess traffic. Rep. Paul Ryan (R-WI) was the most indicated recipient.

Mailing your ashes isn't hard. All you need is an urn, a lot of bubblewrap, a strong box, and a good friend. Plus, of course, you have to die.

Carved in Stone

LEONARD MATLOVICH
A GAY VETERAN OF VIETNAM
WHEN I WAS IN THE MILITARY,
THEY GAVE ME A MEDAL FOR KILLING TWO MEN
AND A DISCHARGE FOR LOVING ONE.

JOHN HEATH
TAKEN FROM COUNTY JAIL & LYNCHED BY BISBEE MOB IN TOMBSTONE
FEB. 22, 1884

ANDREW J. OLSZAK
1895—1979
ABANDONED IN OLD AGE BY WIFE AND CHILDREN
MAY GOD BE MORE UNDERSTANDING AND MERCIFUL

HERE LIES LESTER MOORE
FOUR SLUGS FROM A 44
NO LESS
NO MORE

RODNEY DANGERFIELD
THERE GOES THE NEIGHBORHOOD

Robert Clay Allison
1840—1887
He Never Killed a Man that Did Not Need Killing

Dawn Under

Here lies my wife
I bid her Goodbye
She rests in peace
And now so do I.

Russell Larsen

Two things I love most, Good Horses and Beautiful Women,
and When I Die, I Hope They Tan this Old Hide of Mine
and Make It into a Ladies Riding Saddle,
So I Can Rest in Peace between the Two Things I Love Most.

Bill Kugle

Jan. 20, 1925—Dec. 27, 1992
He Never Voted for Republicans and Had Little to Do with Them

William Shakespeare

Good Friend for Jesus Sake Forbeare,
To Dig the Dust Enclosed Heare.
Blese Be Yᴇ Man that Spares Thes Stones,
And Curst Be He that Moves My Bones.

Here Lies an Athiest.
All Dressed Up and No Place to Go

Merv Griffin

I will Not Be Right Back after the Message
July 6, 1925—August 12, 2007

JESSE JAMES

MURDERED BY A TRAITOR AND A COWARD

WHOSE NAME IS NOT WORTHY TO APPEAR HERE

LUDOLPH VAN CEULEN

3.14159265358979323846264338327950

STUDS TERKEL

CURIOSITY DID NOT KILL THIS CAT

JOEL H. CHESKIN

JULY 23, 1942—FEB. 5, 2014

"AT LAST A HOLE IN ONE"

CAST A COLD EYE

ON LIFE, ON DEATH.

HORSEMAN PASS BY.

W.B. YEATS

JUNE 13TH 1865—JANUARY 28TH, 1939

EDWARD ABBEY

NO COMMENT

DEATH AND THEREAFTER

To qualify as a Near-Death Experience (NDE), the memory of a patient resuscitated from a clinically dead state should include at least a few of the following:

1   Time speeds up or slows down.

2   Thought-processes speed up.

3   A return of scenes from the past.

4   A sudden insight or understanding.

5   A feeling of peace or pleasantness.

6   A feeling of happiness or joy.

7   A sense of harmony or unity with the universe.

8   Confrontation with a brilliant light.

9   The senses feel more vivid.

10   An awareness of things going on elsewhere, as if by extrasensory perception (ESP).

11   Experiencing scenes from the future.

12   A feeling of being separated from the body.

13   Experiencing a different, unearthly world.

14   Encountering a mystical being or presence or hearing an unidentifiable voice.

15   Seeing deceased or religious spirits.

16   Coming to a border or point of no return.

A study in the Netherlands, published in The Lancet, found that 62 of 344 resuscitated cardiac arrest patients in ten Dutch hospitals reported a Near-Death Experience. That's 18 percent. Forty-one of them—12 percent of the total—had a "core experience." The degree of the NDE was scored on a scale by interviewers listening for certain experiences.

These experiences were:

1   Awareness of being dead.

2   Positive emotions.

3   Out of body experience.

4   Moving through a tunnel.

5   Communication with light.

6   Observation of colors.

7   Observation of a celestial landscape.

8   Meeting with deceased persons.

9   Life review.

10   Presence of border.

Six percent of the total scored from one to five, meaning they had superficial NDEs, that is, only slight memories from the time when they were clinically dead. Twelve percent scored from six to ten because they had "core experiences." Seven percent had "very deep NDEs," scoring above ten on the scale.

Near Death Dream

This anecdote comes from an article, "Do 'Near-Death Experiences' Occur Only Near-Death?—Revisited," written by Glen O. Gabbard, M.D. and Stuart Twemlow, M.D., published in *Human Sciences Press*

> A marine sergeant was instructing a class of young recruits at boot camp. He stood in front of a classroom holding a hand grenade as he explained the mechaniscs of pulling the pin to detonate the weapon. After commenting on the considerable weight of the grenade, he thought it would be useful for each recruit to get a "hands-on" feeling for its actual mass. As the grenade was passed from private to private, one 18-year-old recruit nervously dropped the grenade as it was handed to him. Much to his horror, he watched the pin become dislodged as the grenade hit the ground. He knew he had only seconds to act, but he stood frozen, paralyzed with fear. The next thing he knew, he found himself traveling up through the top of his head toward the ceiling as the ground beneath him grew farther and farther away. He effortlessly passed through the ceiling and found himself entering a tunnel with the sound of wind whistling through it. As he approached the end of this lengthy tunnel, he encountered a light that shone with a special brilliance, the likes of which he had never seen before. A figure beckoned to him from the light,

and he felt a profound sense of love emanating from the figure. His life flashed before his eyes in what seemed like a split second. In the midst of this transcendent experience, he suddenly realized that the grenade had not exploded. He felt immediately "sucked" back into his body.

Much to his surprise, the sergeant had picked up the grenade and was chuckling to himself at the reaction of the panic-stricken recruits. It had not occurred to the young soldier that the grenade was only a "dummy" used for demonstration purposes.

The report presents the anecdote as evidence that it is not necessary to be near death to have a Near-Death Experience. The expectation of death may be enough, suggesting that the NDE is merely a psychological event. But the report also cites cases of small children who experience NDEs even though they have no concept of death or previous knowledge of what such an experience is "supposed" to be like.

Hell To Pay

Consider the use of Hell Money. It won't buy much on this side of the Hereafter, but a relative on the other side might need it to bribe Yanluo, a rather nasty god who presides over a place a hell of a lot like Purgatory. Yanluo—also known as Yan and Yama—is so bad that he oversees the Ten Kings of Hell. He passes judgment on the dead, condemning them to Hell for as long as their evil actions in life warrant. Yanluo can reach into the world of the living and inflict warnings on people through such messages as illness, old age, injury. He has a book in which the death date of every person is noted, including the dates of the living.

Like everyone else, Yanluo can always use a little more cash, and he's not above accepting it from new arrivals. For this reason, Buddhists and people in cultures with strong Buddhist traditions burn facsimiles of money as a funeral rite for deceased family members who might need a bribe to shorten or mitigate their sentence. The Hell Money, also known as joss paper, might also be used for any expenses that come up in the Hereafter.

The dead frown on tightfistedness among their survivors, so Hell Money is bought in stacks of very large denominations. Some individuals, due to their guilt or wealth, may need several notes of $5 billion. Sacrifices across a city can produce so much smoke that it becomes a pollution problem. The traditional braziers are now fitted with covers that prevent the escape of ash.

The term "Hell Money" is reputed to have originated with Christian missionaries who taught Orientals that Hell is where non-Christians go after they die.

Soul Survivor

Semi-barbarians on the outskirts of early Greece believed that the soul and the body have a tenuous and uncomfortable relationship. The soul, they believed, was divine, immortal, and longing for freedom. Unfortunately, most of the time it is held in bondage within a body. The only way it can escape is if the body dies. Alas, the escape is brief. It is soon reincarnated in yet another corporeal prison. Orpheus, supposedly the one who thought this up and formalized the Orphic religion, said that permanent liberation can happen only after the soul has advanced through a series of ever-purer bodies. Lives of piety and purity allow the soul to move upward toward godliness, a state of everlasting liberation and life.

Pherecydes of Syros picked up the idea and passed it on to Pythagoras, he of the famous hypotenuse and many other formulations. The idea made its way to Plato almost a century later. Plato wrote about it in The Republic, but it isn't clear whether he believed it to be literally true or simply an allegory of good advice.

The Roman Virgil picked up the idea of metempsychosis, preserving it long enough to be written about by John Donne, Edgar Allan Poe, Herman Melville, Guy de Maupassant, Arthur Schopenhauer, Kurt Gödel, Marcel Proust, Friedrich Nietzsche, James Joyce, Thomas Pynchon, Don DeLillo, David Foster Wallace, and Glenn Alan Cheney.

What King Tut Took

Egyptian Pharao "King Tut" Tutankhamun was buried with a wealth of "funerary objects" meant to ease his transition into the Great Beyond. Among the items were a gold coffin, little coffinettes, boxes, chests, jewels, a gilded throne, other thrones, little statues, a gold, 22-lb. face mask with a sad, tranquil expression, two magical trumpets with the ability to start a war, an alabaster chalice in the shape of a lotus blossom, food, wine, sandals, a dagger with an iron-nickel blade made from a meteorite, and, yes, of course, a change of underwear.

Brief Thoughts on the Inevitable

By the sweat of your face you shall eat bread, till you return to the ground, for out of it you were taken; for you are dust, and to dust you shall return.

Genesis 3:19

Death is nothing, but to live defeated and inglorious is to die daily.

Napoleon Bonaparte

Even death is not to be feared by one who has lived wisely.

Buddha

One death is a tragedy; one million is a statistic.

Joseph Stalin

People fear death even more than pain. It's strange that they fear death. Life hurts a lot more than death. At the point of death, the pain is over.

Jim Morrison

The boundaries which divide life from death are at best shadowy and vague. Who shall say where the one ends, and where the other begins?

Edgar Allan Poe

Art is the tree of life. Science is the tree of death.

William Blake

Remembering that I'll be dead soon is the most important tool I've ever encountered to help me make the big choices in life. Because almost everything—all external expectations, all pride, all fear of embarrassment or failure—these things just fall away in the face of death, leaving only what is truly important.

Steve Jobs

If you die, you're completely happy and your soul somewhere lives on. I'm not afraid of dying. Total peace after death, becoming someone else is the best hope I've got.

Kurt Cobain

Death is not extinguishing the light; it is only putting out the lamp because the dawn has come.

Rabindranath Tagore

I don't fear death so much as I fear its prologues: loneliness, decrepitude, pain, debilitation, depression, senility. After a few years of those, I imagine death presents like a holiday at the beach.

Mary Roach

Life is hard. Then you die. Then they throw dirt in your face. Then the worms eat you. Be grateful it happens in that order.

David Gerrold

My fear was not of death itself, but a death without meaning.

Huey Newton

If we don't know life, how can we know death?

Confucius

The stroke of death is as a lover's pinch, which hurts and is desired.

William Shakespeare

Which death is preferable to every other? The unexpected.

Julius Ceasar

Death is the distant sound of thunder at a picnic.

W.H. Auden

The only difference between death and taxes is that death doesn't get worse every time Congress meets.

Will Rogers

Death and life have their determined appointments; wealth and honor depend on heaven.

Confucius

Death is no more than a turning of us over from time to eternity.

William Penn

Death must be so beautiful. To lie in the soft brown earth, with the grasses waving above one's head, and listen to silence. To have no yesterday, and no to-morrow. To forget time, to forget life, to be at peace.

Oscar Wilde

Life asked death, 'Why do people love me but hate you?' Death responded, 'Because you are a beautiful lie and I am a painful truth.

Author unknown

It is the secret of the world that all things subsist and do not die, but retire a little from sight and afterwards return again.

Ralph Waldo Emerson

They say you die twice. One time when you stop breathing and a second time, a bit later on, when somebody says your name for the last time.

Banksy

Death is a black camel which kneels at the gates of all.

Abdelkader ibn Muhieddine

Call no man happy till he is dead.

Æschylus

Our bodies are prisons for our souls. Our skin and blood, the iron bars of confinement. But fear not. All flesh decays. Death turns all to ash. And thus, death frees every soul.

Darren Aronofsky

Men fear death, as children fear to go in the dark; and as that natural fear in children is increased with tales, so is the other.

Francis Bacon

I have often thought upon death, and I find it the least of all evils.

Francis Bacon

It's better to sit than to stand, it is better to lie down than to sit, but death is best of all.

Indian proverb

Supremus ille dies non nostri extinctionem sed commutationem affert loci. That last day does not bring extinction to us, but change of place.

Cicero

Death makes everything useless.

Rubem Alves

Unbeing dead isn't being alive.

Edward Estlin Cummings

Love is the cousin of death, and the conqueror of death, even if it's slain (and it is slain) in every instance of love.

Carlos Drummond de Andrade

It's the end of life that gives life a chance.

Stephen Jenkinson

I am the resurrection and the life. The one who believes in me will live, even though they die, and whoever lives by believing in me will never die.

Jesus

The last enemy to be destroyed is death.

1 Corinthians 15:26

A time to be born, and a time to die; a time to plant, and a time to pluck up what is planted...

Ecclesiastes 3:2

Modernity has transferred death from the home, the place of love, to institutions, the places of power.

Rubem Alves

Death is simply a shedding of the physical body, like the butterfly coming out of a cocoon.

Elisabeth Kuebler-Ross

Death is not the end.
Death can never be the end.
Death is the road.
Life is the traveller.
The soul is the guide.

Sri Chinmoy

Every door may be shut but death's door.

Chinese Proverb

Death is an art, like everything else.

Sylvia Plath

Expressions for Death and Dying

Buy the farm

Pay the ultimate price

Push up the daisies

Look up at the grass

Ride the pale horse

Shuffle off one's mortal coil

Turn up your toes

Kick the bucket

Shit the bed

Meet your maker

In the box

Cross over

Pass away

Pass over

Go to the happy hunting ground

Bite the dust

Croak

Assume room temperature

Breathe your last

Cash in your chips

Cross the Jordan

Depart this life

Drop like flies

Give up the ghost

Go to a better place

Go bung (Australian)

Bow out

Pull the chain

Flip the switch

Do yourself in

Go the way of all flesh

Kiss your ass good-bye

Take a dirt nap

To have your number up

Go up to the spirit in the sky

No longer suffer

Fall off your perch

Food for worms

Go belly up

Glenn Alan Cheney

Famous Last Words

Tellulah Bankhead (on being asked if she wanted anything): "Codeine...bourbon..."

Bob Marley: "Money can't buy life."

Alexander Graham Bell: "No."

Peter Abelard (philosopher and theologian): "I don't know."

Karl Marx: "Last words are for fools who haven't said enough."

Todd Beamer (passenger on United Flight 93 on Sept. 11, 2001): "You guys ready? Let's roll."

Private First Class Edward H. Aherns (surrounded by dead Japanese soldiers): "The bastards tried to come over me last night. I guess they didn't know I was a Marine."

Leonardo da Vinci: "I have offended God and mankind because my work did not reach the quality it should have."

Benedict Arnold: "Let me die in the old uniform in which I fought my battles for freedom, May God forgive me for putting on another."

Alex (an African grey parrot): "You be good. See you tomorrow. I love you."

Lady Nancy Astor (awakening on her deathbed): "Am I dying or is this my birthday?"

Humphrey Bogart: "I should never have switched from scotch to martinis."

Charles Darwin: "I am not the least afraid to die."

Johannes Brahms (upon sipping a bit of wine): Ah, that tastes nice. Thank you."

Marie Antoinette (after stepping on the foot of her executioner): "*Pardonnez-moi, monsieur. Je ne l'ai pas fait exprès.* (Pardon me. I did not do it on purpose.)"

Richard Feynman: "I'd hate to die twice. It's so boring."

Willem Arondeus (Dutch member of anti-Nazi resistance): "Let it be known that homosexuals are not cowards."

Thomas Edison (looking out the window): "It's very beautiful out there."

Raphael (the painter): "Happy..."

John Wilkes Booth: "Useless...useless..."

Leonard Nimoy (his last tweet): "A life is like a garden. Perfect moments can be had, but not preserved, except in memory. LLAP."

Jane Austen: "I want nothing but death."

Max Baer: "Oh God, here I go!"

Siddartha Gautama Buddha: "Decay is inherent in all things. Be sure to strive [for Nirvana] with clarity of mind."

Queen Elizabeth I: "All my possessions for a moment of time."

Bing Crosby: "That was a great game of golf, fellers."

W.C. Fields: "Goddam the whole fucking world and everyone in it except you, Carlotta."

Bobby Fischer: "Nothing soothes pain like human touch."

James French (being led to the electric chair): "Hey, fellas! How about this for a headline for tomorrow's paper? 'French Fries'!"

Bob Hope (on being asked where he'd like to be buried): "Surprise me."

Steve Jobs: "Oh wow. Oh wow. Oh wow."

Terry Kath: "Don't worry...it's not loaded."

Timothy Leary: "Beautiful."

Wolfgang Amadeus Mozart: "The taste of death is upon my lips...I feel something that is not of this earth."

Marco Polo: "I have not told half of what I saw."

Charles Schulz: "Charlie Brown, Snoopy, Linus, Lucy...how can I ever forget them?"

General John Sedgwick: "They couldn't hit an elephant at this distance!"

George Washington: "I am just going. Have me decently buried and do not let my body be into a vault in less than two days after I am dead. Do you understand me?... Tis well. I die hard, but I am not afraid to go."

Theodore Roosevelt: "Please put out the light."

John F. Kennedy (responding to "You certainly can't say Dallas doesn't love you, Mr. President."): "No, you certainly can't."

Mohandas Gandhi: "Oh, God."

Lady Diana Spencer: "My God, what's happened?"

Poetic Notions

Although Death walks beside us on Life's road,

A dim bystander at the body's start

And a last judgment on man's futile works,

Other is the riddle of its ambiguous face:

Death is a stair, a door, a stumbling stride

The soul must take to cross from birth to birth,

A grey defeat pregnant with victory.

Sri Aurobindo, from Savitri

A telling analogy for life and death:

Compare the two of them to water and ice.

Water draws together to become ice,

And ice disperses again to become water.

Whatever has died is sure to be born again;

Whatever is born comes around again to dying.

As ice and water do one another no harm,

So life and death, the two of them, are fine.

Han Shan

Do Not Stand at My Grave and Weep

Do not stand at my grave and weep

I am not there; I do not sleep.

I am a thousand winds that blow,

I am the diamond glints on snow,

I am the sun on ripened grain,

I am the gentle autumn rain.

When you awaken in the morning's hush,

I am the swift uplifting rush

Of quiet birds in circled flight.

I am the soft stars that shine at night.

Do not stand at my grave and cry,

I am not there; I did not die.

Mary Elizabeth Frye

Rumination

When I can hold a stone within my hand
And feel time make it sand and soil, and see
The roots of living things grow in this land,
Pushing between my fingers flower and tree,
Then I shall be as wise as death,
For death has done this and he will
Do this to me, and blow his breath
to fire my clay, when I am still.

Richard Eberhart

Glenn Alan Cheney

Let's talk of graves, of worms, and epitaphs;

Make dust our paper and with rainy eyes

Write sorrow on the bosom of the earth,

Let's choose executors and talk of wills:

And yet not so, for what can we bequeath

Save our deposed bodies to the ground?

Our lands, our lives and all are Bolingbroke's,

And nothing can we call our own but death

And that small model of the barren earth

Which serves as paste and cover to our bones.

Shakespeare, *Life and Death of Richard the Second*

To-morrow, and to-morrow, and to-morrow,

Creeps in this petty pace from day to day

To the last syllable of recorded time,

And all our yesterdays have but lighted fools

The way to dusty death.

Out, out, brief candle!

Life's but a walking shadow, a poor player

That struts and frets his hour upon the stage

And then is heard no more: it is a tale

Told by an idiot, full of sound and fury,

Signifying nothing.

Shakespeare, *Macbeth*

Death

Rainer Marie Rilke

Before us great Death stands
Our fate held close within his quiet hands.
When with proud joy we lift Life's red wine
To drink deep of the mystic shining cup
And ecstasy through all our being leaps—
Death bows his head and weeps.

Death Be Not Proud

John Donne

Death be not proud, though some have called thee
Mighty and dreadful, for, thou art not so,
For those whom thou think'st, thou dost overthrow,
Die not, poor death, nor yet canst thou kill me.
From rest and sleepe, which but thy pictures bee,
Much pleasure, then from thee, much more must flow,
And soonest our best men with thee doe goe,
Rest of their bones, and soules deliverie.
Thou art slave to Fate, Chance, kings, and desperate men,
And dost with poyson, warre, and sicknesse dwell,
And poppie, or charmes can make us sleepe as well,
And better than thy stroake; why swell'st thou then?
One short sleepe past, wee wake eternally,
And death shall be no more; death, thou shalt die.

Because I Could Not Stop for Death

Emily Dickenson

Because I could not stop for Death —
He kindly stopped for me —
The Carriage held but just Ourselves —
And Immortality.

We slowly drove — He knew no haste
And I had put away
My labor and my leisure too,
For His Civility —

We passed the School, where Children strove
At Recess — in the Ring —
We passed the Fields of Gazing Grain —
We passed the Setting Sun —

Or rather — He passed Us —
The Dews drew quivering and Chill —
For only Gossamer, my Gown —
My Tippet — only Tulle —

We paused before a House that seemed
A Swelling of the Ground —
The Roof was scarcely visible —
The Cornice — in the Ground —

Since then — 'tis Centuries — and yet
Feels shorter than the Day
I first surmised the Horses' Heads
Were toward Eternity —

Children's Fearless Hearse Song

Did you ever think, when the hearse goes by
That you might be the next to die?
 They'll wrap you up in a clean white sheet,
And put you down about six feet deep
They put you into a wooden box,
And cover you over with earth and rocks.
It's not so bad for the first few weeks,
Until your coffin begins to leak.
The worms crawl in, the worms crawl out,
The worms play pinochle on your snout.
They eat your eyes, they eat your nose,
They eat the jelly between your toes.
They eat your clothes, they eat your hat,
They crawl in skinny, and crawl out fat.
Your teeth fall in and your eyes pop out,
Your brains come trickling down your snout.
Then you turn disgustingly green.
Your skin as slimy as whipping cream.
So whenever you see the hearse go by,
Watch out! You...may...be...
the...next...to...*die*!

Glenn Alan Cheney

Dirge Without Music

Edna St. Vincent Millay

I am not resigned to the shutting away of loving hearts in the hard ground.
So it is, and so it will be, for so it has been, time out of mind:
Into the darkness they go, the wise and the lovely. Crowned
With lilies and with laurel they go; but I am not resigned.

Lovers and thinkers, into the earth with you.
Be one with the dull, the indiscriminate dust.
A fragment of what you felt, of what you knew,
A formula, a phrase remains,—but the best is lost.

The answers quick and keen, the honest look, the laughter, the love,—
They are gone. They are gone to feed the roses. Elegant and curled
Is the blossom. Fragrant is the blossom. I know. But I do not approve.
More precious was the light in your eyes than all the roses in the world.

Down, down, down into the darkness of the grave
Gently they go, the beautiful, the tender, the kind;
Quietly they go, the intelligent, the witty, the brave.
I know. But I do not approve. And I am not resigned.

Do Not Go Gentle into that Good Night

Dylan Thomas

Do not go gentle into that good night,
Old age should burn and rave at close of day;
Rage, rage against the dying of the light.

Though wise men at their end know dark is right,
Because their words had forked no lightning they
Do not go gentle into that good night.

Good men, the last wave by, crying how bright
Their frail deeds might have danced in a green bay,
Rage, rage against the dying of the light.

Wild men who caught and sang the sun in flight,
And learn, too late, they grieved it on its way,
Do not go gentle into that good night.

Grave men, near death, who see with blinding sight
Blind eyes could blaze like meteors and be gay,
Rage rage against the dying of the light.

Friendship

Ralph Bergengren

I have a friend. If I should die
I know he would sit down and cry.

The sun would shine, the sky be blue,
And birds would sing just as they do

In trees and bushes every day,
But I would not be there to play.

And so I know there'd be no game
That ever could be quite the same.

For that is just the way that I
Would feel if he should go and die.

THE MERRY BURIAL BLOG

Arboreal Burial

Connecticut Green Burial Grounds is unique in that it allows a chosen tree to be planted over a grave. In a short time, the sapling's roots tap into the body below. Nutrients from that body become the tree.

If you could be a tree, what tree would you like to be? What characteristics would you like to become?

Would you like to be an oak—black, white, red, scarlet, pin, live, scrub, swamp, overcup, chestnut, chinkapin, which?—tall and strong, symbol of endurance, the stuff of the hull of the Mayflower, the species where the Charter of Connecticut once hid?

Or are you more the maple type, lush in summer, glorious in fall, flush with sweet sap, the tree kids most prefer to climb?

Perhaps you'd like to be reborn into magnificence, a beech with overarching foliage as big as a house, a stout trunk of silver where lovers carve their hearts.

You could be a linden, ever-so aromatic, beloved by bees, seeds favored by chipmunks, known by friends as basswood, quick to grow, going up a hundred feet to blossom in the sun.

Why not for once be slender and beautiful, a stem or pair of stems of birch—white with bark that burns hot, black that tastes a minty sweet, paper all covered with curls—your leaves serrate, petiolate, stipulate, and feather-veined? In winter you would be beautiful in snow.

Or would you sum your life as a weeping willow, your hair hung low around your grave, the space around you cavernous and cool? With every breeze you'd sway a slow and lovely dance.

Or are you evergreen—cedar, hemlock, spruce or pine? Or ash or elm, chestnut, cherry, hawthorn, hickory, sassafras, mulberry, sycamore, or gum?

So many trees to choose from, but you only get one.

Frequently Asked Questions on Posthumous Matters

Must I embalm my loved-one?

No. No state laws in the United States require embalming. Some states require embalming or refrigeration if the body is not buried or cremated within a reasonable period of time. Some require embalming if the body is to be on public display. Immediate burial with no such treatment is always an option.

Is there such a thing as "Bring Your Own" coffin?

Yes. Under rules established by the Federal Trade Commission, you are allowed to buy or even make a coffin, casket, shroud or urn. They are available on the Internet from many sources. You can have the container shipped straight to the funeral home. You don't have to be there when it arrives, although the funeral home may ask you to inspect the casket. You will not have to pay anything to the funeral home for using a unit bought elsewhere.

What's the difference between a casket and a coffin?

A casket is essentially a rectangular box, though some are oval. The traditional coffin has sloped shoulders.

What is a green casket?

A green casket or coffin is made entirely of biodegradable materials, with no nails, synthetic glues, paint, varnish, or synthetic cloth. Common materials include bamboo, hemp, wool, cotton, cork, teak, willow, rattan, seagrass, banana leaves, and organic cardboard.

Is a coffin necessary for cremation?

No, though many states require a rigid container for cremation.

Do I need to buy a cemetery plot before I die?

No, but if you have a preferred place, you'd best buy it beforehand. You can contact a cemetery directly, or you can ask a funeral home to help. In some cases the cemetery is operated by a church or cemetery association (such as Connecticut Green Burial Grounds), in some cases a municipality.

Is there such a thing as a used/rental casket?

Yes. A funeral home can rent you a nice but previously occupied casket from which the interior has been removed and replaced for each previous occupant. These caskets are usually used for viewing or a funeral service. Afterward the deceased can be removed to a more affordable or appropriate unit.

Can I get a casket emblazoned with the icons and trademarks of the band known as Kiss?

Yes. See memorials.com. Click on "Unique Caskets." Other options are the names and logos of sports teams, even the ones that suck. Your funeral home of choice can help you with your unique wishes.

How much does a coffin cost?

The sky's the limit! And so is the ground. A tricked out upper-end casket of mahogany with all the bells and whistles can cost $20,000 or more. An average range of funeral home offerings start around $700 and goes up from there. A cardboard casket made of 25-35% recycled material produced in a bleach-free process and held together by a starch-based glue can be had for $300. Caskets of organic woven fibers such as banana leaf, willow, seagrass, or rattan, cost between $1,500 and $3,000. A simple pine box can be had for around $1,000. Plus, of course, if there's anything as inevitable as death and taxes, it's shipping and handling, but that's between the buyer and seller, not the funeral home.

What's cool about a cardboard casket?

People can write messages on it. Children can draw pictures on it. It blots up tears and it cycles into the ecosystem more quickly than other materials.

Can I be buried in my back yard?

Maybe, but it's extremely complicated. The rules vary from state to state. Generally, if a Zoning and Health Department approves, you can do it. But wherever you are, you're going to need a very large yard, a very good lawyer, and a very cooperative Zoning Department and Health Department.

Is burial at sea an option?

Sure! Anchors aweigh! But you have to be at least 3.5 miles from shore and the water has to be at least 600 feet deep. The body and any container must be prepared to sink directly. A funeral director will know the rules, which are determined by whichever state has jurisdiction. Of course if you're in international waters, you can do whatever you want. U.S. Navy veterans and their dependent families are entitled to burial at sea at no cost.

If I'm so fortunate as to kick the bucket in the Nutmeg State, can Connecticut Green Burial Grounds handle all my funeral arrangements?

No. As a cemetery association, CGBG can offer only the plot, the burial, maintenance of the burial ground, and burial records. By law (in Connecticut) a certified funeral director must sanitize the body and certify proper burial. A funeral home must also handle transportation and necessary permits and paperwork.

On Grief

The well known Five Stages of Grief is also called the Kübler-Ross Model, named after Swiss psychiatrist Elisabeth Kübler-Ross. The "stages" apply to the terminally ill, the survivors of deceased loved ones, and people afflicted with other types of trauma, such as drug addiction, incarceration, and divorce. They can also be observed in sports fans whose team loses and in supporters of political candidates who lose elections.

Kübler-Ross later regretted calling the five emotional states "stages" because the grieving do not necessarily move through an orderly series. They may skip some, may bounce back and forth among two or more, remain mired in one.

The stages she identified are:

• Denial—when the grieving individual believes the prognosis or other unacceptable cause of grief is not correct or cannot be true.

• Anger—when denial is not longer possible, the individual questions the injustice of the trauma, seeks to blame others, or blames and lashes out at others.

• Bargaining—an attempt to avoid or reverse the cause of grief by offering a personal sacrifice or promising painful change of lifestyle.

• Depression—the despair of feeling there is no hope, no point in continuing life, no reason to do anything, especially anything social.

• Acceptance—a sensation of calmness and sedated satisfaction as the individual accepts the inevitable and resigns to its immutable reality.

Subsequent scientific research has questioned the identifiable existence of these states or any inevitable progression from denial through acceptance. Many environmental factors, such as information, resources, emotional support, previous experience, the cause of the grief, and overlapping griefs or problems, can influence the movement between states. Though some of the scientific community has relegated the model to fallacy, it can be useful in understanding one's own or someone else's emotional states. Burial—the ritual as well as the consignment to the earth—may contribute to acceptance, which is often the best possible outcome for grief.

Heuristic Quiz on Your Afterlife

Which ice cream best represents death?

a.   plain vanilla

b.   rocky road

c.   melted

d.   double pickle

e.   java mint chip cookie dough with whipped cream, chocolate sauce, crushed nuts, and a cherry on top

f.   dirt (-flavored)

Which of these reincarnated entities would you prefer to become?

a.   a puppy

b.   a kitten

c.   a redwood tree

d.   a sperm whale

e.   a presidential tapeworm

f.   a babe in the Black Hole of Calcutta

Which kind of person is most likely to be reincarnated as a gypsy moth?

a.   slimeball toadies

b.   yellow-bellied backstabbers

c.   slicked-back evangelicals

d.   pot-bellied congressional sellouts

e.   timber rustlers and their ilk

f.   stinkers of ill repute

What do you figure's at the end of the Great White Tunnel?

a.   72 virgins

b.   your mother

c.   St. Peter

d.   The Prince of Darkness in a bridal gown

e.   an immigration official

f.   a gleaming, dazzling, whistling sphincter

Which makes most sense about the reincarnation deal?

a. You get what you deserve but never know why.

b. You are assigned a random life form somewhere between amoeba and zebra.

c. You become the tree that taps into your posthumous nutrients.

d. You end up back where you were before you were born— Nowheresville.

e. Next time you will read the instructions.

f. Your life will be the opposite of what it is this time around.

Where can you find answers about the afterlife?

a. The Bible

b. The Talmud

c. The Oracle at Delphi

d. The Merry Burial blog

e. Written on the subway walls

f. The twilight tootle of a wood thrush

Which would be your preferred afterlife?

a. Eternity in a paradise of unrelenting bliss.

b. Haunt the earth, able to see but not touch.

c. Take your chances at a random human rebirth.

d. The oblivion of nonexistence.

e. Become a leprechaun with the power to influence lives.

f. Take all your possessions to an ethereal gated community of the rich and famous.

Would you rather return as...

a. a man or a woman?

b. a Mexican or a Palestinian?

c. a swamp oak or a coconut palm?

d. a police dog or a widow's cat?

e. the child of a Democrat or a Republican?

f. Charlemagne, Jesus, Hefner, Trump, or Liberace?

Which are advantages of green burial?

    a.   You return to nature what nature is due.

    b.   Your survivors will have a shady spot to remember you in.

    c.   It beats burning 28 gallons of fossil fuel and contributing to the misery of upcoming generations.

    d.   You will be remembered for your wisdom, not your greed.

    e.   You will at last have done something right.

    f.   Your death will exemplify your life.

Which will have the biggest impact on your afterlife destiny?

    a.   your virtues

    b.   your sins

    c.   your suffering

    d.   dumb luck

    e.   the way you were buried

    f.   your deathbed confessions

Speaking of deathbed confessions, you'd best list a few before it's too late.

    a.

    b.

    c.

    d.

    e.

    f.   Other

The Sad, Green Burial of the Pilgrims at Plymouth

The Pilgrims of Plymouth had to resort to a particularly sad burial practice during their first winter in the New World. Due to complications getting underway back in England, they didn't arrive at Plymouth until the middle of November, 1620. It was too late to find a place to live and build houses to get them through the winter. A hundred and two passengers had to spend the next several months in their tight, cold, damp quarters on the gun deck of the Mayflower. Sharing the space with a small sail boat, a few cannons, some farm animals, and bundles of carry-on luggage, they barely had enough room to all lie down at the same time.

In December they started to take sick. They thought it was scurvy, but it was more likely influenza or pneumonia. It afflicted everyone. They were so weak they could hardly get up. When individuals died, they spent days right where they were, right next to people suffering the same symptoms the newly deceased had suffered. William Bradford and Myles Standish were among the few who were able to do anything about the dead.

Removing the corpses was a challenge. They had to be hauled up onto the main deck, then lowered into a boat that could be rowed to shore. It's also possible the bodies were passed out through small portholes on the gun deck that would have been used for cannon fire in the event of attack.

The landing craft was too big to actually reach the sandy shore. Those assigned burial duty had to wade the last few yards through the frigid winter water of Cape Cod Bay, dragging the bodies after them.

Since it was winter, the ground beyond the beach was frozen solid. The only alternative was a sandy hill just above the beach, where the sand could be easily dug. So there they opened the graves, and not very deep. "Six feet under" wasn't a requirement then any more than it is today. And of course it would have been impossible to build coffins. Impossible. It's unlikely the bodies were even wrapped in a shroud.

There were Indians in the area, and in one skirmish shortly after the Mayflower arrived, the Americans and immigrants exchanged gunfire and a barrage of arrows. The Pilgrims had reason to worry, and by January they had reason to hide the fact that they were dying off at a rapid rate. So once a dearly departed had been laid to rest, the burial crew smoothed off the sand to make it look like plain, unconsecrated beach. Nothing marked the spot, not even a cross. By spring, nobody knew exactly who was where. Not that it mattered. Their bodies were to be at one with nature, their souls departed to wherever it was that Pilgrim souls went.

Stuff to Know about Cremation

First of all, it isn't spelled *creamation* any more than the process takes place at a *creamery*. It takes place in a *cremator*, which is an industrial furnace at a *crematory*, which is the business end of a *crematorium*. But it's where you end up if you get creamed by a car, asteroid, or ice cream truck, so the confusion is understandable.

Creamers are fake cream. A cremulator is a machine that pulverizes incinerated remains. Some cremulators are like blenders, others like grinders. Either way, it takes a good twenty minutes, and the results are the same: four to six pounds of remains, perhaps a little more for individuals who spent too much time chowing down at a creamery. These scant pounds represent just 3.5 percent of the human body. The other 96.5 percent is blowing in the wind.

It's considered politically incorrect to call the remains "cremains," which is seen as slangily disrespectful of the person they used to be. "The cremated remains of the late So-and-So" is preferred. "Ashes" in the same phrase would be also acceptable even if technically inappropriate. Anything resembling ash has been incinerated into smoke. What remains has the color and consistency of sand from a beach where nobody wants to go.

A word of caution: certain implants must be removed prior to cremation. It is the funeral director's job to see that this happens. A pacemaker can explode so powerfully that it could damage the cremator, even injure people standing nearby. Other little bombs in the body include spinal cord stimulators, bone nails, and implanted drug reservoirs. Breast implants are not a problem. Titanium hips, tooth fillings, and other metals must be separated after cremation lest they damage the cremulator.

Cremation offers a few advantages over burial. It's less expensive than embalming, vaults, caskets, a burial plot, and the interment process. Cremated remains are a lot easier to transport than whole bodies. And generally speaking, survivors can cast the ashes close to home or in an appropriate place.

Cremation is not as environmentally benign as some believe. Bodies are cremated individually, each requiring the burning of some 28 gallons of fuels during the 90- to 120-minute process. The combustion releases some 540 pounds of carbon dioxide into the atmosphere of an overheating planet. Embalmed bodies release chemical residues, and even the unembalmed release whatever toxins, such as heavy metals, the body accumulated during a lifetime in a polluted environment. Some but not all of these toxins are captured by abatement equipment. If a casket is incinerated along with the body, it, too, may release vaporized chemicals. The trees that died for the casket's wood will not be generating oxygen, and their combusted carbon contributes to global warming. In the case of mahogany and certain other fine woods, the trees may have been taken from a rainforest and shipped thousands of miles.

Natural burial is the most benign means of posthumous disposal. No fossil fuels are burned except in transporting the body to the grave site. (Some cemeteries offer a horse-drawn carriage for this trip.) The body is hastened into the ecosystem. Heavy metals and other corporeal contaminants remain in the ground, in many cases rendered harmless by decomposition and plant uptake. The body, its clothes, and the casket or shroud, all of biodegradable material, soon become a plant or animal. Who knows, maybe they will become grass, and then a cow might eat it and turn it into cream. And there you go: creamation. Maybe it should be a word after all.

Posthumous Preferences

Close your eyes. Imagine you're dead. You've been privileged to receive a green burial. A tree has been planted above you, and it's already taken you up and grown large enough to be of interest to squirrels, birds, and people in need of shade. Your spirit hovers nearby, waiting to see your family and friends come around to visit, remember, and celebrate.

But you know how some of your friends are. And some of your extended family, too. They're all visiting with the best of intentions and the fondest of memories, but some of them could probably use a list of rules—the dos and don'ts of graveside behavior.

So which of these (subject to sexton approval) would go on the Please Do side of your list, which on the Please Don't?

• Carve your name in my bark.

• Scatter native wildflower seeds all around me.

• Pick one wildflower and take it home.

• Yank up any bittersweet, loosestrife or poison ivy that arises.

• Burn a tire right here over my dead body.

• Pour a libation of decent wine into the ground.

• Leave a tidy pile of litter for somebody else to pick up.

• Take home a nut, fruit, or leaf that fell from me.

- Make love, right here.

- Leave a pile of peanuts for the squirrels.

- Lean against me and take a selfie.

- Take a group picture with everybody in it.

- Spend the night.

- Remain totally sober.

- Talk to me.

- Climb me.

- Eat my toadstools.

- Ask the sexton if you can hang a bird house on me.

- Detonate thunderous fireworks.

- Take pictures of me in summer, fall, winter, spring.

- Slow-dance on my grave.

- Bury something small, biodegradable and symbolic under an inch of soil.

- Leave a bouquet of plastic flowers in a styrofoam pot.

- Do that special thing you do: paint, knit, sing, write, sculpt, tinker, whatever...

- Park right here next to me and change your oil.

- Do something illegal that doesn't hurt anybody.

- Write me a letter.

- Read a poem with my eyes.

- Listen to a bird and imagine that's me reminding you of something.

- Spread out a blanket and have a picnic with your friends.

- Get to know my neighbors.

- Spray pesticides all over the place.

- Smell my soil.

- Forgive yourself.

- Forgive me.

- Pray.

- Laugh.

- Cry.

- Whine.

- Try to explain this to a small child.

Wake Up, America!

Buried alive? You've got a real problem and not much time to solve it. If you've been embalmed, of course, your problems are over. You are more than dead. Not even a worm would eat you. You're going to be more than dead for a long, long time.

But if you should find yourself in the situation of awakening in a coffin, first ask yourself how you know you're in a coffin and not just some dark, horizontal telephone booth. Do you remember dying? If so, odds are you aren't in a coffin. You're in bed and you're asleep and having a bad dream. Try waking up.

If waking up doesn't work, try going to sleep. That will minimize your consumption of oxygen. You'll live longer. And then die. Like everybody else. Just be glad you weren't embalmed.

But you may be too excited to fall asleep. Who could blame you? It's like your first day on a new job. You're confused. You're nervous. You want to do things right, but you haven't received proper training. They're thrown you into a new situation, and you've hit the ground running. Or in this case, lying down.

Relax. You've got enough oxygen for a couple of hours. You'll wake up in time. Because really, you're just dreaming all this.

With a little luck you'll dream you were buried with your cell phone. This is far more likely than being buried alive. Of course it's also likely your battery's dead. (That's why they buried it with you! Ha, ha—just a little coffin humor.) Of course if you were so fortunate as to have received a green burial—which may be why you weren't embalmed—they wouldn't bury you with a phone, not unless it's organic.

But maybe they forgot it was in your pocket, and the battery is no deader than you, and you aren't in a concrete vault six feet under, just four feet under and no vault, and in an organic cardboard casket in a cemetery not far from a cell tower. Try calling 9-1-1, see if they believe you. Then call the most dependable person you know who owns a shovel or, better yet, a backhoe. Tap your head gently on the bottom of the coffin, and then harder and harder as you listen to the detailed instructions on how to leave a message. Make sure you mentiont that you're leaving the message *after* the funeral.

Try texting. Text your entire list of contacts. And pray—pray that you aren't doing this in your sleep. Which you probably are. And they will never let you forget. And for the rest of your life, you're going to wish you were dead. And someday you will be—hopefully before you're buried.

Acknowledgements

The author offers deep thanks to Elizabeth Foley, of Connecticut Green Burial Grounds, for her inspiration and contribution to this work. Special thanks are also due to Senior Editors Denise Dembinski and Ralph Cheney for their literary attentions.

Glenn Alan Cheney

GLENN ALAN CHENEY is the author of more than thirty books of fiction and nonfiction, hundreds of articles, and a good number of op-eds, short stories, and poems. He has also translated or edited translations of several books by Brazilian authors. He has taught at various colleges and universities in Connecticut, where he lives with his wife, Solange. He is a trustee of Connecticut Green Burial Grounds.

www.ingramcontent.com/pod-product-compliance
Lightning Source LLC
Chambersburg PA
CBHW032115280326
41933CB00009B/853